Bartholomew's Comet

By Alan Trussell-Cullen

Illustrated by Jon Davis

Dominie Press, Inc.

Publisher: Raymond Yuen
Project Editor: John S. F. Graham
Editor: Bob Rowland
Designer: Greg DiGenti
Illustrator: Jon Davis

Published by:

℗ Dominie Press, Inc.

1949 Kellogg Avenue
Carlsbad, California 92008 USA

www.dominie.com

1-800-232-4570

Paperback ISBN 0-7685-1816-4
Printed in Singapore by PH Productions Pte Ltd
1 2 3 4 5 6 PH 05 04 03

Table of Contents

Chapter One
Breakfast with Dad

Our house is always crazy at breakfast time. Everyone is rushing around getting ready.

The only calm ones are Dad and me.

We sit at the table, reading the newspaper. Dad reads one part of the paper. I read another.

Sometimes, Dad will lean over and show me an article. One day he showed me a news item about Bartholomew's comet.

"Look at this, Jake," Dad said. "It's coming back again."

"Where?" I said.

"Here. To our solar system," said Dad. "Maybe tonight. It's like Halley's comet, only Halley's comet comes to our solar system every *seventy-six* years. Bartholomew's comet arrives every *thousand* years."

"Then I guess you weren't around when it came last time," I said.

Dad looked over the top of the newspaper and grinned.

"Nope," he said. "But, I'm glad I wasn't. Usually when Bartholomew's comet

comes, all kinds of bad things happen.
That's why some people call it the
unlucky comet."

"What kinds of things?" I asked.

"The usual disasters," he said.
"Earthquakes, storms, tidal waves,
volcanoes erupting. Things like that.
The last time it came around, there were
fires and famines all over the world.
According to what the paper says, it's
coming closer than last time. Our little
planet is going to pass right through its
tail. How about that!"

"Does that mean the disasters will be
even worse this time?"

"Could be," said Dad.

Chapter Two
The Disasters Begin!

It didn't take long for the disasters to start. First, I got a detention for talking in class when I wasn't talking at all! (Jerome was doing all the talking—I was just listening!)

Then I got a mushy note from Belinda

Parker. Well, actually, it was a note asking if I'd like to go to a school dance with her. Of course, I had to show it to my best friend, Jerome.

"Hey," Jerome said. "That's a real love note you've got there. Obviously she's madly in love with you!"

"Don't tell anyone!" I said.

Of course, he did. And that person told someone else. And they told someone else. And in no time at all, the Grunge heard about it!

The Grunge is the school bully, and he thinks all the girls are in love with him. (They aren't!) His real name is Dennis, but no one calls him that. (At least, not to his face!) When he heard about Belinda and the note, he started telling everyone he was going to throw me in the lake unless Belinda went to the dance with him!

I really wanted to go to the dance with Belinda, but I didn't want to end up in the lake. It was more likely that I would be in the lake, because the Grunge is much bigger than I am!

To keep out of his way during lunch, I snuck off to the school library. No one goes to the library much at our school— everyone's afraid of our librarian! I assumed I wouldn't bump into the Grunge there. And I didn't.

Instead, I bumped into Belinda!

"Hi," I said, trying to sound cool. "I uh... I got your note."

"Yeah, and I heard about the Grunge," she said. "I'll understand if you don't want to go to the dance with me. I'm not going with *him*! I think I'll just stay home. Maybe we could do something else another time?"

I should have been smart and said, "Thanks, Belinda. Sure, another time!"

But did I? No, I didn't! Instead, I had to be all brave and stupid and say, "I'm not afraid of the Grunge! I'd love to go to the dance with you!"

Chapter Three
The Mystery Rock

I might have impressed Belinda, but now I was in serious danger from the Grunge! I took the long way home through the city park, just to avoid seeing him.

And that's how I came across the

strange rock.

It was lying in the grass as though it had fallen out of the sky. It was about the size of a hamburger, and it was bright blue.

I bent down to pick it up. That's when I got my first big surprise. I expected it to be heavy. After all, rocks usually are. But it had no weight at all. It just sort of floated in my hand. And what was weirder still was that it seemed to make me feel light! I don't know why, but I suddenly gave it a little squeeze.

Wow! Shock-time Arizona!

It was as though I was lifted off the ground by a tornado. One minute I was standing on the ground, and the next minute I was banging my head on a branch near the top of a tree.

I looked down at the ground way below me.

"Now what?" I thought.

I started to loosen my grip on the rock. Suddenly, I found myself plunging down toward the ground!

"Yikes!" I yelled, and in my terror I squeezed the rock again. I shot up like a beach ball that someone's been holding under water!

Bang! I hit my head against that same branch again!

"OK," I thought to myself. "So it obviously has something to do with the pressure. So this time, I started to *slowly* loosen my grip on the rock. And I began to *slowly* descend.

When I squeezed a bit more, I stopped and hovered in midair.

I leaned forward and gave the rock a bit of a squeeze. Whoosh! I shot forward like a pea out of a peashooter!

"Whoa!" I said, as I straightened up again and came to a halt. "I can fly!"

Once I was back on the ground again, I had a good, hard look at this amazing rock. What was this magic force? Why was it in the park? And most importantly, why was it blue?

And then I remembered Bartholomew's comet. Maybe that was where this rock had come from.

Chapter Four
Splash! Splash!

The next morning at school, the disasters began all over again. I opened up my desk, and inside was a note written on a piece of grubby paper. And this wasn't a love note!

To Jake the bellyache,

Meet me at the lake after school... Or Else!

The Grunge

Jerome said I should tell the teacher, but I thought that would only get me in more trouble. And besides, I'd been thinking about the rock and my flying lessons. Maybe I could use that to make the Grunge leave me alone.

I looked up. The Grunge was looking my way. He gave me a nasty grin and whispered, "Splash! Splash!"

As soon as school was out, I rushed to the lake. I wanted to get there early so I could get in a little more flying practice before anyone else arrived.

I was kind of surprised when I took the rock out of my pocket. It seemed smaller. It was now about the size of a baseball. I gave it a quick squeeze, and instantly I was airborne. Everything worked just fine. In fact, I even did some graceful dives and twirls. I was thinking about trying a loop, when I heard footsteps—someone was coming. I quickly landed and got ready to meet the Grunge. The rock had shrunk again—I could close my hand around it now. I hoped it was still big enough for me to use it more

The Grunge turned up with a crowd of his friends.

"Talking to the ducks?" he asked.

I was scared stiff, but I tried to look cool.

"Look," I said. "This is just dumb. Belinda doesn't want to go to the dance with you. So why don't we just shake hands and be friends?"

The Grunge and his friends all roared with laughter at this.

But the Grunge said, "All right. I'll shake hands with you..."

He held out his hand. He was grinning in a nasty way.

"Come on!" said the Grunge. "Are you afraid to shake hands with me?"

He suddenly reached forward and grabbed my hand. Then he squeezed it with all his might!

It just happened to be the hand that was holding the rock. Suddenly we both shot up into the air. Everyone gasped.

"Yikes!" the Grunge yelled. "What the... What's happening?!"

"I'm taking you on a little tour of the lake," I said. I leaned forward and squeezed the rock. I managed to

maneuver us past the lakeshore and above the water. There we were, hovering over the lake. The Grunge let go of my hand and grabbed my shirt in terror.

"I... What's going on? Put me down!" the Grunge spluttered.

"I don't think so," I said.

"OK, OK. Take it easy," he said, looking down at the water. "I don't know how you're doing this, but please put me down." Then he whispered, "I'm afraid of heights."

"First you have to promise to stop bullying everyone," I said.

"OK! I promise! I promise!" said the Grunge.

"And you have to try to be nice to people for a change!"

"I'll try! I'll try!"

The others were gaping up at us. But I

was beginning to worry about the rock. In my hand it felt no bigger than a little pebble. I didn't want us both to end up in the lake when the rock disappeared completely. So I gave it one more squeeze and leaned forward to bring us back to shore again.

"Wow!" one of the boys said.

"That was a cool trick!" said another.

"How did you do it?"

I couldn't tell them about the rock or my theory that it had come from Bartholomew's comet.

So I said, "I spend a lot of time in the library, you know. I found this magic spell in one of the books. The only trouble is, I can't remember the spell. I can't even remember the title of the book."

"Come on," one of them said. "A

book?"

"It's true," I said. "Go look it up."

The other boys looked at each other, then left for the library. I don't think they knew it was closed after school let out.

The Grunge stayed behind. "Whatever that was, don't do it again. I won't bother you anymore, just don't put any magic spells on me, OK?"

"OK," I said. "And I won't tell anyone that you're afraid of heights."

I quickly switched the pebble to my other hand and offered to shake hands with him. This time, he didn't squeeze so hard.

The next day, the Grunge and his friends spent almost the whole day in the library to see if they could find the book! The librarian was amazed. She'd never seen so many kids in the library.

Chapter Five
The School Dance

The school dance turned out to be a good time. Belinda and I had fun. The Grunge went, too. He volunteered to help our teacher run it, and he brought along his own CDs for the music. Everyone said how the Grunge seemed to be different. He was actually being nice to people!

After the dance, Jerome, Belinda, and I and some of our friends all walked home together.

"I wish I could have seen your amazing flying trick," said Jerome. "Why don't you show us how you did it?"

I put my hand in my pocket. I felt what was left of the rock. It was now no bigger than a jelly bean!

"My magic spell only lasts so long," I said. "There's probably only enough magic to fly one person."

"Oh, pick me!" begged Belinda. "After all, I *did* write you a love note!"

And she winked at Jerome.

Everyone laughed, and I could feel myself blushing.

"OK," I said. I put the little pebble in

one hand and took Belinda's hand with the other.

"Hold on!" I said. And I gave the pebble a squeeze.

Slowly, Belinda and I lifted off the ground. It was a very shaky flight, and we only went up about five feet. Belinda gasped. Her eyes were huge. She was hardly breathing!

"Awesome!" she whispered.

I could feel the pebble shrinking fast. It felt like it was fizzing in my hand.

"We have to go down," I said.

Belinda nodded.

We drifted down and fell the last few feet.

"Amazing!" said Belinda. "How did you do it?"

I opened my hand to show Belinda the rock, but it had disappeared.

While everyone else was cheering, I whispered into her ear, "Magic!"

"Look!" said Belinda. She was pointing up into the night sky. "I thought I saw a shooting star. But it's gone now."

"Probably Bartholomew's comet," I said. "It won't be back for another thousand years now."

The next morning, Dad and I were reading the newspaper again.

"Looks like Bartholomew's comet didn't have much of an effect after all," said Dad.

"Not much," I said, with a small grin.